**Illustrators:**
Keith Vasconcelles
Agi Palinay

**Editor-in-Chief:**
Sharon Coan, M.S. Ed.

**Editor:**
Walter Kelly, M.A.

**Art Directior:**
Elayne Roberts

**Cover Artist:**
Keith Vasconcelles

**Product Manager:**
Phil Garcia

**Imaging:**
Rick Chacón

**Research:**
Bobbie Johnson

**Publishers:**
Rachelle Cracchiolo, M.S. Ed.
Mary Dupuy Smith, M.S. Ed.

# SCIENCE
## in a
# BAG
### PRIMARY

**Author:**
Evan D. Forbes, M.S. Ed.

*Teacher Created Materials, Inc.*
P.O. Box 1040
Huntington Beach, CA 92647
©1995 Teacher Created Materials, Inc.
Made in U.S.A.

**ISBN-1-55734-197-4**

# Table of Contents

# Table of Contents (cont.)

## Physical Science

### Simple Machines

### Simple Chemistry

### Electricity and Magnetism

### Miscellaneous

# Introduction

Primary age students quickly move beyond their own personal areas to broaden their sense of place. It is now becoming increasingly important to provide this group of children with new insights about their communities and to help them make connections to the larger world of which they are a part. Providing a solid curricular base of literature, of math, of science, of real-life lessons about real families, and of events in other times and places is essential.

## What Is Science in a Bag?

Welcome to the exciting world of hands-on science. *Science in a Bag* offers students and their families the opportunity to explore science together, a process much different from the conventional teaching methods of science in today's classroom. Science can be a stimulating topic if approached in the correct way. When everyday science skills are connected to a student's understanding of the world around them, interest in science (as well as classroom scores) will begin to rise.

This book has been written with several purposes in mind. In place of repeated paper-pencil homework assignments, *Science in a Bag* offers thought-provoking alternatives. First, you will find intriguing activities that involve the student's entire family. Second, you will find activities relating to the world around you, reinforcing basic science skills and promoting real-life problem solving. Finally, you will find follow-up classroom activities to tie in homework, extend its boundaries, stimulate science discussions, challenge students, and bring science studies to life for your students.

# How to Use This Book

## Using a Pre-formatted Science Experience:

- Choose one of the pre-formatted science experiences.
- Select a date the science experience is due and write it on the activity form for your students.
- Each science experience is set up in an easily reproducible form. A copy should be made for each student.
- There will be an asterisk (*) next to each material you will need to supply.
- Place an activity sheet inside each science kit and give one to each student.
- Have students take science kits home and complete their assignments.
- When the science kits have been returned, use the follow-up activities created especially for the science experience you chose.

## Creating Your Own Science Experience:

- Use the "Ideas for Creating Your Own Science Experience" provided in the back of this book to make your own science experiences.
- Select the experiences that best fit the age, interests, and ability level of your students.
- List the purpose, materials, procedure, explanation, introduction, and follow-up of the experience on blank science experience forms provided on pages 78-79.
- Include a date due on your activity form.
- Each science experience is set up in easily reproducible form. A copy should be made for each student.
- Place an asterisk (*) next to each item you will supply.
- Place an activity sheet inside each science kit and give one to each student.
- Have students take science kits home and complete their assignments.
- When the science kits have been returned, provide follow-up activities based on the science experience sent home. The follow-up activities already in this book will provide some excellent suggestions for you to follow.

# Science Experience Suggestions

Providing take-home science experiences for your class will be educational, exciting, and fun.  Here are a few helpful suggestions before you begin.

- Have students take home the introductory letter to parent/guardian, found on page 7.  This letter clearly explains how the science experiences will be conducted.  As well as promoting excitement for this new activity, the letter should answer any questions parents/guardians may have.

- Send home the supply request letter (page 8) asking for whatever materials may be needed.  Parents should be eager to supply the materials needed for the science experiences.

- Recycle the materials used whenever possible.  Encourage your students to care for and return their science kits after each science experience is complete.

- Allow approximately 4-7 days for your students to complete their science experience.  It is best if the time period includes a weekend. This will allow your students to involve their entire family.

- Spend time discussing with students what they think about their science experience before beginning the follow-up activities.

- Plan ahead so there will be plenty of time to complete a science experience.

- Use the awards that have been provided to recognize students who show exceptional enthusiasm and dedication.  Special awards have been included for students who complete experiences that were especially difficult.

# Letter Home

Dear Parent/Guardian,

This week, I will be assigning our _____take-home science experience.  It promises to be an exciting activity that will include your entire family.

On _____, your child will receive a science kit to take home.  This kit will include the materials and procedure for completing the assigned activity.  In some cases it may be necessary to use items from around the house to complete the activity.  You and other family members are encouraged to help your child with the science experience.

This science experience will motivate your child to think about and discuss science outside the classroom.  It will reinforce science skills learned in the classroom, as well as encourage problem solving.  It will provide a practical application of science in real life.  And finally, the science experience will provide an unusual homework activity the whole family is sure to enjoy.

This take-home science experience will be due on _____.  Before your child brings the science kit back to school, please sign the activity form in the space provided.

Once the science kits have been brought back to school, we will follow up with a variety of hands-on activities involving what was done at home.  All items used from home will be returned at the end of the day following their use.

Watch for more exciting science experiences in the weeks to come.  I am confident that you will enjoy these unusual, challenging activities as much as your child.

Sincerely,

# Supply Request Letter

Dear Parents,

Our class will be involved in many take-home science experiences this year. Could you help make these experiences a success by looking around your house for the items listed below? If so, please send them with your child as soon as possible.

Thank You!

# The Rub

**Date Due:** _____

**Directions:** Answer the questions about your tree observations. Then glue or tape your rubbings in the space provided.

Student's Name: _____

Parent's Signature: _____

✂ - - - - - - - - - - - - - - - - - - - - - - - - - - - - - - - - - - -

# The Rub

**Purpose:** To make observations about the bark, branches, and leaves of a tree.

**Materials:**
- pencil
- glue or transparent tape
- scissors
- paper (tissue or tracing preferred)*
- neighborhood tree
- student activity sheet*

**Procedure:**
1. Go out into your neighborhood and choose a tree you like, preferably one where you can reach the branches and leaves.

2. Once you have chosen a tree, make the following observations and write them down on your activity sheet. How tall is your tree? How big is the trunk of your tree? What does your tree smell like? What does your tree feel like? How old do you think your tree is?

3. When you have made all your visual observations, take a piece of paper and a pencil and make a rubbing of the bark, a branch, and a leaf.

4. Then, using your scissors cut out each rubbing and glue or tape it to your attached activity sheet in the space provided. Label each rubbing.

5. Return your completed activity sheet and any school supplies on the date due.

# The Rub (cont.)

## Introduction and Follow-up Activities

### Setting the Stage

- Discuss with students what observation skills are and the importance of practicing them, especially when studying science.

- Prior to assigning their take-home investigation, have students practice their observation skills in class.

- Pass out activity sheets to your students and review with them what they will be investigating at home.

### Extensions

- Review with students the results of their home investigations.

- Have students make several more rubbings of bark or leaves, labeling each rubbing, and then make a booklet of those rubbings.

- Take students on a walk around the schoolyard and make observations about the plants and trees you see.

- Have a tree specialist (botanist) come to your class to talk about the differences in trees.

### Closure

In a journal, have students write down in a few sentences what they learned from participating in this investigation.

### Related References

Arnosky, Jim. ***Crinkleroot's Guide to Knowing Trees.*** Macmillan, 1992. (2-4)

Bond, Ruskin. ***Cherry Tree.*** Boyds Mills, 1991. (PS-3)

Brandt, Keith. ***Discovering Trees.*** Troll LB, 1982. (1-3)

Fowler, Allan. ***It Could Still Be a Tree.*** Children's LB, 1990. (1-2)

Izen, Marshall and Jim West. ***Why the Willow Weeps: A Story Told with Hands.*** Doubleday, 1992. (K-3)

Suess, Dr. ***The Lorax.*** Random LB, 1971. (K-3)

# Plant Parts

**Date Due:** _____

**Directions:** Draw a picture and then explain in your own words what happened during your investigation.

Student's Name: _____

Parent's Signature: _____

---

# Plant Parts

**Purpose:** To learn to recognize and identify the different parts of a plant.

**Materials:**

- paper lunch bag*
- large piece of construction paper*
- white glue or transparent tape
- student activity sheet*

**Procedure:**

1. Write your name on the outside of your lunch bag.

2. Find an area outside or near your house where you have permission to collect samples of plant parts (i.e., root, stem, leaf, flower, and seed).

3. Fold your piece of construction paper in half. Using tape or glue, attach the five plant parts you collected to the left side of the fold. Label your plant parts.

4. Complete the attached activity sheet and glue or tape it to the right side of your construction paper. Then return it and any unused school supplies on the date due.

# Plant Parts (cont.)

## Introduction and Follow-up Activities

### Setting the Stage

- Prior to this activity, discuss the different parts of plants with your students (roots, stems, leaves, flowers, and seeds). Be sure they have seen and can recognize a variety of examples of each plant part.

- Have a class discussion about respect for living things.

- Discuss with your class safe ways to collect plants.

- Pass out science kits and explain to students what they will be investigating at home.

### Extensions

- Review with students the results of their home investigations.

- Have students compare what they found with others in the class. Things to look at are pointed or rounded leaves, smooth or rough bark, seed size and weight, and flower petal color.

- After students finish comparing their plant parts. Have them go on a scavenger hunt to find specific things.

### Closure

In a journal, have students try to identify the plants from which they got their plant parts.

### Related References

Challand, Helen J. *Plants Without Seeds.* Children's LB, 1986. (2-4)

Mahy, Margaret. *The Pumpkin Man and the Crafty Creeper.* Lothrop LB, 1991. (K-3)

Rahn, Joan Elma. *Seven Ways to Collect Plants.* Atheneum, 1978. (all)

Silverstein, Shel. *The Giving Tree.* Harper & Row, 1964. (all)

Taylor, Barbara. *Green Thumbs Up!: The Science of Growing Plants.* Random House, 1992. (all)

Wexler, Jerome. *Flowers, Fruits, and Seeds.* Simon & Schuster, 1991. (1-3)

# Against Gravity

**Date Due:** _____

**Directions:** Draw a picture and then explain in your own words what happened during your investigation.

Student's Name: _____

Parent's Signature: _____

✂ - - - - - - - - - - - - - - - - - - - - - - - - - - - - - - - - - - - - - - - - - - - - - - -

# Against Gravity

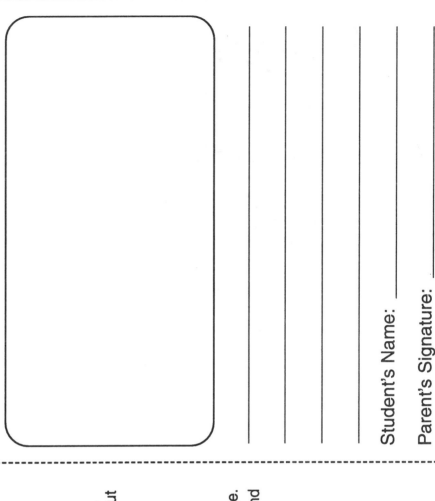

**Purpose:** To show how water rises in plants.

**Materials:**
- one white carnation*
- two drinking cups (clear)
- two different colors of food coloring*
- scissors
- student activity sheet*

**Procedure:**

1. Using your scissors, trim the stem of your carnation. Then, carefully split the carnation stem, leaving about 2" (5 cm) below the flower uncut.

2. Fill both plastic cups 1/2 way with water.

3. Add a few drops of food coloring to each cup. One color per cup.

4. Place half of the stem in each of the colored cups.

5. Let stand for a few hours. Then, observe the change.

6. Complete the attached activity sheet and return it and any school supplies on the date due.

**Why:** Everyone knows plants receive food and water through their roots. This is possible because of capillary action—the ability of water to flow against the pull of gravity by passing in and out of tiny plant cells packed closely together. The same process can be seen by dipping a paper towel in water.

# Against Gravity (cont.)

## Introduction and Follow-up Activities

### Setting the Stage

- Prior to students doing their home investigations, bring in and share an assortment of plants with differing stems—cactus, fern, rose, tulip, etc. Have students examine the different stems and write down their observations to be shared with the class.

- Have students inspect several cut strips of celery. They should look for traces of moisture and how celery receives its nutrients.

- Pass out science kits and explain to students what they will be investigating at home. Before leaving class, have them make predictions. Either create a class list or have students individually write their predictions in a journal, as to how food and water rise in plants.

### Extensions

- Review with students the results of their investigations. Then compare their pre-investigation predictions with their final results and compare and discuss the differences, if any.

- Have students repeat this investigation with other stemmed plants. Have them observe any differences between the new stemmed plants and the carnation.

- Have students use celery to test a plant's need for water. They should remove a piece of celery from the water for 24 hours and then compare it to a piece of celery that remained in the water. Then place the celery back into the water for 24 hours and note any further changes.

- Have a florist come to your class to discuss methods of coloring and keeping flowers fresh.

### Closure

In a journal, have students write down or draw a picture of their thoughts regarding this investigation.

### Related References

Ardley, Neil. ***The Science Book of Things That Grow.*** Harcourt, 1991. (3-5)

Wexler, Jerome. ***Flowers, Fruits, and Seeds.*** Simon & Schuster, 1991. (1-3)

***Plants.*** (Series: What's Inside) Dorling, 1992. (all)

# Seedless Plants

**Date Due:** _____

**Directions:** Draw a picture and then explain in your own words what happened during your investigation.

Student's Name: _____

Parent's Signature: _____

---

# Seedless Plants

**Purpose:** To show that some plants can grow without seeds.

**Materials:**

- a potato
- an onion
- two glass jars, wide enough for an onion and potato to fit inside
- several toothpicks*
- water
- two containers filled with potting soil
- a knife
- student activity sheet*

**Procedure:**

1. Fill both glass jars with water.
2. Insert toothpicks into each vegetable and suspend them from each of the glass jars. At least 1/4 of each vegetable should be covered in water.
3. Keep the jars filled with water.
4. When the shoots begin to grow and are at least 1" (2.5 cm) long, use a knife to cut out a chunk of each vegetable, with the shoots still attached.
5. Plant each shoot in a container and cover completely with potting soil, and then water.
6. Continue to water the containers each day and observe.
7. Complete the attached activity sheet and return it and any unused school supplies on the date due.

**Why:** Plants are able to grow without seeds through a process called vegetative propagation. These plants regenerate themselves using a part of the plant that already exists. Not all plants have this capability.

# Seedless Plants (cont.)

## Introduction and Follow-up Activities

### Setting the Stage

- Have students share their knowledge of plants (i.e., growth, visual differences, land vs. water, etc.).

- After students have shared what they know, fill in the missing areas. Review with them the plant life cycle (seed to plant to seed).

- Allow students to see plants growing in different ways. Pictures from books or CD-ROM should provide a good source.

- Pass out investigation sheets and explain to students what they will be investigating at home.

### Extensions

- Review with students the results of their home investigations.

- Either in class or at home, have students try growing other plants with different plant parts.

- Ask students how this process of growing plants can be used in today's society.

### Closure

In a journal, have students write an imaginative story about plants growing from parts other than seeds. Give them the option to illustrate their stories.

### Related References

Challand, Helen J. *Plants Without Seeds.* Children's LB, 1986. (2-4)

Hall, Howard. *The Kelp Forest.* Blake Publishing, 1990. (all)

Handelsman, Judith F. *Gardens from Garbage: How to Grow Indoor Plants from Kitchen Scraps.* Millbrook, 1993. (3-5)

Petrich, Particia and Rosemary Dalton. *The Kid's Garden Book.* Nitty Gritty Productions, 1974. (all)

Taylor, Barbara. *Green Thumbs Up!: The Science of Growing Plants.* Random House, 1992. (all)

Watts, Bame. *Potato.* Silver LB, 1988. (all)

# Life in a Bottle

**Date Due:** _____

**Directions:** Draw a picture and then explain in your own words what happened during your investigation.

Student's Name: _____

Parent's Signature: _____

---

# Life in a Bottle

**Purpose:** To create a self-contained artificial environment for plants.

**Materials:**

- 2-liter plastic bottle
- soil
- water
- student activity sheet*
- gravel or small rocks
- small plants found outside
- scissors

**Procedure:**

1. Remove the label and cut the bottle in two about 1/4 of the way up from the bottom.

2. In the top portion, where it is cut away from the bottom, cut six vertical 1" (2.5 cm) slits spaced around the bottle.

3. Fill the plastic base of your bottle with gravel and small rocks.

4. Take the bottom of your bottle to a wooded area around your house. Dig up a few small plants, keeping the roots intact. Place the plants you collect (along with some soil from the same area) in the bottom of your bottle.

5. Water the soil and seal your plants by replacing the top portion of the bottle, fitting the slits down over the base.

6. Place in a well-lit area and observe your terrarium for several days.

7. Complete the attached activity sheet and return it and any unused school supplies on the date due.

# Life in a Bottle (cont.)

## Introduction and Follow-up Activities

### Setting the Stage

- Review with your students what plants need to have in order to grow. This might also be a good time to review the water cycle.

- Have students define what the word *terrarium* means. Afterwards, show them several different types of terrariums. Model the construction of a bottle terrarium from a two-liter plastic bottle.

- Pass out investigation sheets and explain to students what they will be investigating at home.

### Extensions

- Review with students the results of their home investigations.

- Have students continue to monitor their terrariums and record how long the plants live.

- If the materials exist, you may want your students to create a classroom terrarium. Make sure to have them research what plants and possibly animals would live best inside a terrarium.

### Closure

In a journal, have students write at least three reasons why terrariums would be important to people studying plants.

### Related References

Bjork, Christina. *Linnea's Windowsill Garden.* Farrar, 1988. (1-3)

Krementz, Jill. *A Very Young Gardener.* Dial LB, 1991. (K-3)

Oechsli, Helen. *In My Garden: A Child's Gardening Book.* Macmillan, 1985. (PS-1)

Petrich, Particia and Rosemary Dalton. *The Kid's Garden Book.* Nitty Gritty Productions, 1974. (all)

Sendak, Maurice. *Kenny's Window.* Harper, 1956. (K-3)

Taylor, Barbara. *Green Thumbs Up!: The Science of Growing Plants.* Random House, 1992. (all)

Wilkes, Angela. *My First Garden Book.* Knopf LB, 1992. (2-6)

# Animals at Home

**Date Due:** _____

**Directions:** Fill in the information required about your animal. Then, draw or tape a picture of your animal on the back of this page.

**Animal's name:**

Type of animal: _____

**Group:** *circle one*

amphibian     arthropod     bird         fish

mammal        mollusk       reptile      other? _____

How much food does your animal eat daily? _____

Approximate weight: _____

Approximate size: _____

Number of legs: _____

Body color(s): _____

Body covering (feathers, fur, scales, etc.): _____

Student's Name: _____

Parent's Signature: _____

✂------------------------------------------------------------

# Animals at Home

**Purpose:** To observe and understand the differences of animals found in your home.

**Materials:**

- pencil
- crayons
- pet (can be pet of a friend, neighbor, or relative)
- student activity sheet*

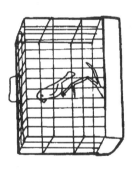

**Procedure:**

1. Chose an animal you want to observe.

2. During this investigation, set aside three separate times you can observe your animal. Each observation period should be at least one hour long.

3. While observing your animal, complete the activity sheet provided.

4. Return your completed activity sheet and any school supplies on the date due.

# Animals at Home (cont.)

## Introduction and Follow-up Activities

### Setting the Stage

- Discuss with students what makes animals different from each other.

- Ask students to come up with a definition for domestic animals and one for wild animals.

- Ask students what they must provide for domestic animals.

- Have a class discussion about why people like to have animals as pets.

- Pass out activity sheets to your students and review with them what they will be investigating at home.

### Extensions

- Have students share the results of their home investigations.

- Have students research a wild animal most closely related to the domestic animal they observed, and then report their findings to the class.

- Set up a day when students can bring to class the animals they observed.

- Invite an animal specialist (veterinarian) to your classroom.

### Closure

In a journal, have students write about how they would take care of an animal if they had one.

### Related References

Broekel, Ray. *Gerbil Pets and Other Small Rodents.* Childern's LB, 1983. (all)

Hausherr, Rosmarie. *My First Puppy.* Macmillan, 1986. (2-4)

Morris, Ann. *Loving.* Lothrop LB, 1990. (PS-2)

Podendorf, Illa. *Pets.* Children's LB, 1983. (2-3)

Selsam, Millicent and Joyce Hunt. *A First Look at Cats.* Walker LB, 1991. (1-3)

Zappler, George and Lizbeth. *Amphibians as Pets.* Doubleday Paper, 1973. (all)

Ziefery, Harriet. *Let's Get a Pet.* Viking, 1993. (PS-3)

# Spider Motel

**Date Due:** _____

**Directions:** Draw a picture and then explain in your own words what you observed during your investigation.

Student's Name: _____

Parent's Signature: _____

---

# Spider Motel

**Purpose:** To create a livable habitat for a spider and then observe it for several days.

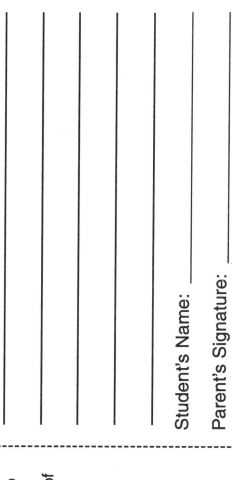

**Materials:**

- large glass jar with lid
- piece of sponge*
- small amount of dirt
- drinking glass
- small piece of cardboard*
- water
- live insects (i.e., flies, mosquitos, moths, etc.)
- student activity sheet*

**Procedure**

1. Fill the bottom of your glass jar with dirt, and add a small stick and a sponge moistened with water. Punch tiny air holes in the lid to allow the spider to breathe.

2. Using your drinking glass and piece of cardboard, go outside in search of a spider. When you find one, place the glass over it and enclose it with the piece of cardboard.

3. Gently place the spider in its new habitat. Remember, use only one spider per jar. (If there are two spiders in one jar, one may eat the other.)

4. Keep the sponge damp with water and frequently provide live insects to keep your spider healthy.

5. Return your completed activity sheet and any school supplies on the date due.

# Spider Motel (cont.)

## Introduction and Follow-up Activities

### Setting the Stage

- Have students define the terms *predator* and *prey*.

- Discuss with students the nature and importance of the predator/prey relationship. Give students some examples of animals that share this symbiotic relationship.

- Create a spider information center, allowing students to familiarize themselves with spiders (don't forget dangerous ones!) before they begin their investigation.

- Pass out science kits and explain to students what they will be investigating at home.

### Extensions

- Review with students the results of their home investigations.

- Have students identify what kinds of spiders they had, gather research on their spiders, and have them present their information to the class.

- Have students make a "Spider Motel" for the classroom and then allow them to take turns caring for a spider and observing how it lives.

### Closure

In a journal, have students write a story about the spider they observed at home or the one in the classroom.

### Related References

Back, Christine. ***Spider's Web.*** Silver Paper, 1986. (K-3)

Bender, Lionel. ***Spiders.*** Watts LB, 1988. (3-4)

Gibbons, Gail. ***Spiders.*** Holiday LB, 1993. (1-2)

Graham, Margaret B. ***Be Nice to Spiders.*** Harper LB, 1967. (PS-2)

Martin, C.L.G. ***Three Brave Women.*** Macmillan, 1991. (K-2)

Parsons, Alexandra. ***Amazing Spiders.*** Knopf LB, 1990. (1-4)

Popendorf, Illa. ***Spiders.*** Children's LB, 1984. (1-4)

Simon, Seymour. ***Pets in a Jar: Collecting and Caring for Small Wild Animals.*** Puffin Paper, 1979. (all)

Souza, D.M. ***Eight Legs.*** Carolrhoda, 1991. (3-5)

# Raptor Diet

**Date Due:** _____

**Directions:** Draw a picture and then explain in your own words what happened during your investigation.

Student's Name: _____

Parent's Signature: _____

✂ - - - - - - - - - - - - - - - - - - - - - - - - - - - - - - - - - - - - - - -

# Raptor Diet

**Purpose:** To determine the types of things birds of prey cannot digest.

**Materials:**

- owl pellet (fumigated), commercially available*
- paper or plastic place mats
- plastic gloves*
- tweezers or forceps (if available)*
- magnifying lens*
- glue
- student activity sheets*

**Procedure:**

1. Cover the area where you will be dissecting your owl pellet.

2. Using your tweezers, forceps, or fingers, separate your pellet and spread its contents in front of you.

3. Examine the things you find with your magnifying lens in order to determine what they are.

4. Group the bones by the categories listed on your activity sheet.

5. When you have found, cleaned, and separated all the bones in your pellet, try to determine what the owl ate.

6. Glue the bones you have collected in the spaces provided or try to reconstruct the animal that was eaten. Good luck!

7. Complete the attached activity sheets and return it and any unused school supplies on the date due.

# Raptor Diet (cont.)

Glue the bones you find in the appropriate places.

### Skull
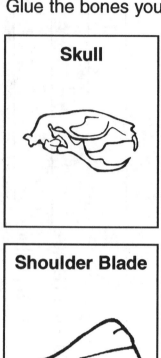

### Jaw
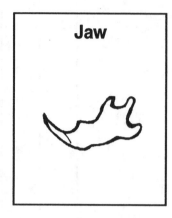

### Completed Skeleton
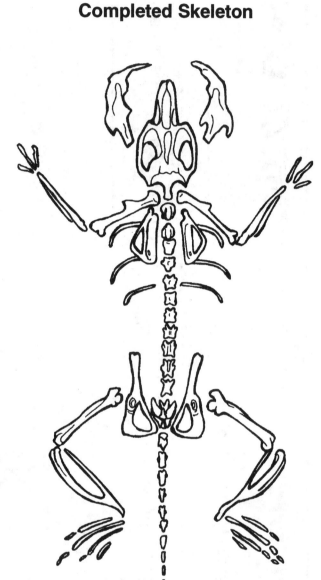

### Shoulder Blade
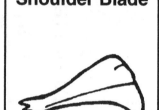

### Vertebrae
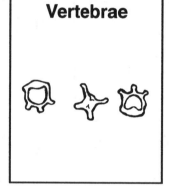

### Ribs
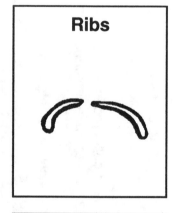

### Hip
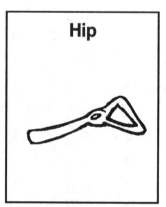

### Foreleg

### Hind Leg
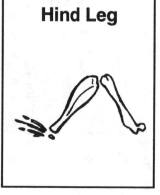

# Raptor Diet (cont.)

## Introduction and Follow-up Activities

### Setting the Stage

- Have students define what the term *raptor* means.

- Formulate a class list of raptors.

- Discuss with students how birds of prey eat and how their digestive processes work.

- Discuss with students what happens to the materials that birds of prey cannot digest.

- Pass out science kits and explain to students what they will be doing during their home investigations.

### Extensions

- Review with students the results of their home investigations.

- Have students research one raptor to find out its eating and digestive habits. Then when they have completed their research, have them try to determine how often they eat and how many animals are found in the average pellet.

- Invite someone who works with raptors to come to class and give a presentation.

### Closure

In a journal, have students comment on what it would be like to cough up in front of other people the things they could not digest.

### Related References

Barrett, Norman. *Birds of Prey.* Watts LB, 1991. (3-5)

Brown, Fern G. *Owls.* Watts LB, 1991. (3-6)

DeWitt, Lynda. *Eagles, Hawks, and Other Birds of Prey.* Watts, 1989. (3-6)

Epple, Wolfgang. *Barn Owls.* Carolrhoda LB, 1992. (3-6)

Lepthien, Emilie U. *Bald Eagles.* Children's LB, 1989. (1-3)

Ling, Mary. *Owl.* Dorling, 1992. (PS-1)

Parry-Jones, Jemima. *Amazing Birds of Prey.* Knopf LB, 1992. (1-4)

# Life Underground

**Date Due:** _____

**Directions:** Draw a picture and then explain in your own words what happened during your investigation.

Student's Name: _____

Parent's Signature: _____

---

# Life Underground

**Purpose:** To create a liveable habitat for earthworms and to then observe them in it.

**Materials:**

- large wide-mouthed clear jar
- clean empty soup can, with one end removed
- potting soil*  • sand*
- vegetable scraps and peels
- black construction paper*
- tape
- earthworms
- student activity sheet*

**Procedure:**

1. Place the tin can, with the closed end facing up, in the middle of the glass jar.
2. Fill the jar with potting soil so it is level with the top of the tin can.
3. Add a thin layer of sand, approximately 1" (2.5 cm) to the top of the soil.
4. Add a few vegetable scraps and peels to the top of the soil.
5. Add water to the soil to moisten; be sure not to overwater.
6. Cover the jar completely with the black construction paper so no light is permitted to get through.
7. Add a few earthworms from the backyard, screw on the lid, and leave for 24 hours.
8. Take off the lid and observe what has happened.
9. Complete the attached activity sheet and return it and any unused school supplies on the date due.

# Life Underground (cont.)

## Introduction and Follow-up Activities

### Setting the Stage

- Have a class discussion to see what students might already know about earthworms.

- Set up a display for your class, showing pictures of some of the different types of worms that exist in the natural world (e.g., flatworms, ribbon worms, roundworms, and segmented worms).

- Pass out science kits and explain to students what they will be investigating at home.

### Extensions

- Review with students the results of their home investigations.

- Review with students the anatomy of an earthworm.

- In a large terrarium, have students create and take care of a worm farm, much in the same manner as their home investigation.

### Closure

In a journal, have students write a story about the life of a worm. Make sure they give their worms names.

### Related References

Bender, Lionel. *Invertebrates.* Watts, 1988. (3-6)

Dorman, N.B. *Petey and Miss Magic.* Shoe String, 1986. (3-5)

Glaser, Linda. *Wonderful Worms.* Millbrook LB, 1992. (PS-2)

Lionni, Leo. *Inch by Inch.* Astor Honor, 1986. (PS-2)

Selsam, Millicent E. *A First Look at Animals Without Backbones.* Walker LB, 1977. (1-3)

# Movin' Around

**Date Due:** _____

**Directions:** Draw a picture and then explain in your own words what happened during your investigation.

Student's Name: _____

Parent's Signature: _____

---

# Movin' Around

**Purpose:** To begin to understand how different types of animals move around.

**Materials:**

- several small rubber bands*
- large balloon*
- stiff plastic (coffee can lid, milk container, etc.)
- large bowl or pan of water
- stapler or paper clips*
- student activity sheets*
- plastic drinking straws*
- scissors
- plastic knife*

**Procedure:**

1. Fill a balloon half way up with water from the tap. Remove the balloon from the tap and hold the opening to keep water from shooting out.

2. Over a sink or bowl, open the balloon enough to stick in a plastic drinking straw to the bottom. Then hold the opening to keep water from shooting out.

3. Using a rubber band, attach the neck of the balloon to the straw, making sure it is tight enough so water will not come out.

4. Bend the remaining part of the straw in half and attach a second rubber band so the straw will stay in place.

5. Cut the plastic into two fishtail-shaped pieces. Place each cut-out tail against the neck of the balloon and attach with a rubber band. Then staple or paper clip the ends of the tail.

6. Put the plastic knife between the two pieces of the tail, with the sharp end facing up. Then place the fish in the bowl or pan.

7. Lightly press your finger against the "nose" of the fish.

28

# Movin' Around

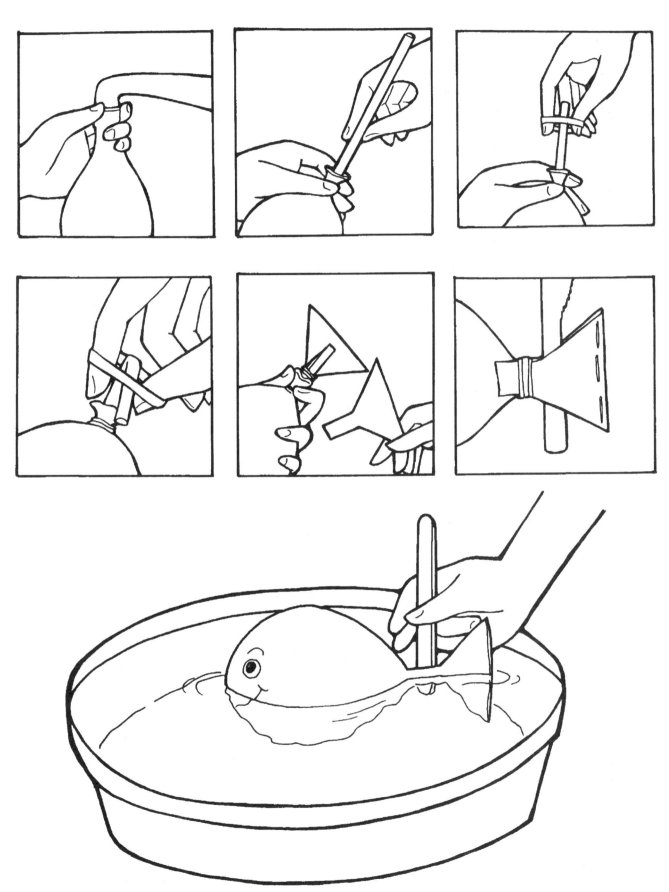

# Movin' Around (cont.)

**Date Due:**_____

**Directions:** Draw a picture and then explain in your own words what you observed during your investigation.

_____

_____

_____

_____

_____

_____

_____

Student's Name: _____

Parent's Signature: _____

# Movin' Around (cont.)

## Introduction and Follow-up Activities

### Setting the Stage

- Ask students all of the different ways animals can move around.

- Discuss with students what would happen if a wild animal were unable to move. What if a domesticated animal could not move?

- Ask students if they know anyone who cannot move because of a disability.

- Pass out science kits and explain to students what they will be investigating at home.

### Extensions

- Review with students the results of their home investigations.

- Have students find out if all fish move in the same manner.

- Have students compare the movement of fish to other aquatic animals and then to land animals.

### Closure

In a journal, have students make a list of all the reasons animals need to move.

### Related References

Cherfas, Jeremy. *Animal Navigators.* Lerner, 1991. (3-5)

Dorros, Author. *Animal Tracks.* Scholastic, 1991. (PS-3)

Evans, Lisa G. *An Elephant Never Forgets its Snorkel: How Animals Survive Without Tools and Gadgets.* Crown LB, 1992. (3-5)

Hornblow, Lenora and Arthur. *Insects Do the Strangest Things.* Random House, 1990. (all)

*Reptiles Do the Strangest Things.* Random LB, 1991. (2-4)

Myers, Arthur. *Sea Creatures Do Amazing Things.* Random LB, 1981. (2-4)

# What's in the Soil?

**Date Due:** _____

**Directions:** Draw a picture and then explain in your own words what happened during your investigation.

Student's Name: _____

Parent's Signature: _____

---

# What's in the Soil?

**Purpose:** To discover and examine things that are living and nonliving in soil.

**Materials:**

- 4' (120 cm) of string*
- small trowel or shovel
- small sealable plastic bag*
- magnifying lens*
- four craft sticks*
- student activity sheet*

**Procedure:**

1. Using your string and craft sticks, go outside, and find a place where you can measure off and mark 1 sq. foot (.09 sq. meters) of soil.

2. Begin at one corner of your marked-off plot and carefully examine the soil.

3. Use your magnifying lens to better view things that are very small.

4. Record all of your observations on your activity sheet.

5. Place a trowel full of soil inside a plastic bag for later study in class.

6. Complete the attached activity sheet and return it and any unused school supplies on the date due.

# What's in the Soil? (cont.)

## Introduction and Follow-up Activities

### Setting the Stage

- Discuss what dirt (soil) is with students.

- Ask students what type of rock is most commonly found in dirt.

- Pass out science kits and explain to students what they will be investigating at home.

### Extensions

- Review with students the results of their home investigations.

- Have students go outside into the school yard and collect samples of dirt. Then have them compare those samples with the samples they brought from home.

- Have a class discussion about the most interesting things, living and nonliving, found in the dirt samples.

### Closure

In a journal, have students draw a picture of the most interesting thing they found.

### Related References

Bourgeois, Paulette. *The Amazing Dirt Book.* Addison Wesley Paper, 1990. (3-5)

Burnie, David. *How Nature Works.* Reader's Digest, 1991. (3-8)

Cole, Joanna. *The Magic School Bus Inside the Earth.* Scholastic, 1987. (2-5)

Fosjer, Joanna. *Cartons, Cans, and Orange Peels: Where Does Your Garbage Go?* Houghton, 1991. (3-6)

Greene, Carol. *Caring for Our Land.* Enslow LB, 1991. (1-3)

McNulty, Faith. *How to Dig a Hole to the Other Side of the World.* Harper LB, 1979. (2-4)

Podendorf, Illa. *Rocks & Minerals.* Children's LB, 1982. (1-4)

Stille, Darlene K. *Soil Erosion and Pollution.* Children's LB, 1990. (1-3)

# Rock Hardness

**Date Due:** _____

**Directions:** Draw a picture and then explain in your own words what you observed during your investigation.

Student's Name: _____

Parent's Signature: _____

✂

# Rock Hardness

**Purpose:** To determine the degree of hardness for various rocks.

**Materials:**

- collection of rocks
- magnifying lens*
- hardness kit—penny, streak plate (unglazed tile), steel nail*
- Mohs' Hardness Scale*
- student activity sheet*

**Procedure:**

1. Choose a rock from your collection.
2. Try to scratch the rock you chose, first using your fingernail, and then the other items found in your hardness kit.
3. After testing your rock, use Mohs' Hardness Scale to determine its degree of hardness.
4. Repeat this process with all the rocks in your collection. Then rank your rocks from softest to hardest.
5. Return your completed activity sheet and any school supplies on the date due.

**Why:** Although rocks have many similar characteristics, this home investigation will show your child how rocks differ in hardness. The hardness often determines how rocks are ultimately used.

34

# Rock Hardness (cont.)

## Mohs' Hardness Scale

from 1 (softest) to 10 (hardest)

### Mineral Examples

| Mineral | Hardness |
|---|---|
| Talc | 1 |
| Gypsum | 2 |
| Alcite | 3 |
| Fluorite | 4 |
| Apatite | 5 |
| Feldspar | 6 |
| Quartz | 7 |
| Topaz | 8 |
| Corundum | 9 |
| Diamond | 10 |

## Hardness Test

| Minerals scratched by: | Are a hardness of: |
|---|---|
| fingernail | 2.5 or less |
| penny | 3 or less |
| glass (streak plate) | 5.5 or less |
| steel nail | 6.5 or less |
| none of the above | greater than 6.5 |

# Rock Hardness (cont.)

## Introduction and Follow-up Activities

### Setting the Stage

- Set up a display center of rocks and minerals for students to examine. Allow students who have rock collections at home to bring in samples and add them to the classroom display.

- Explain to students what Mohs' Hardness Scale is and demonstrate for your class how to determine the degree of hardness of a rock.

- Pass out science kits and explain to students what they will be investigating at home.

### Extensions

- Review with students the results of their home investigations.

- Have students collect their own rocks and test them for their degree of hardness.

- Invite a rock specialist (mineralogist) to your classroom.

### Closure

In a journal, have students draw a picture of each mineral example used in Mohs' Hardness Scale.

### Related References

Challand, Helen J. *Volcanoes.* Children's LB, 1983. (1-4)

Cole, Joanna. *The Magic School Bus Inside the Earth.* Scholastic, 1987. (2-5)

Gans, Roma. *Rock Collecting.* Harper LB, 1984. (1-3)

Hiscock, Bruce. *The Big Rock.* Macmillan, 1988. (1-4)

Kehoe, Micheal. *The Rock Quarry Book.* Carolrhoda, 1981. (2-3)

Kerbo, Ronal. *Caves.* Childerns LB, 1981. (3-5)

Podendorf, Illa. *Rocks & Minerals.* Children's LB, 1982. (1-4)

Selsam, Millicent E. and Joyce Hunt. *A First Look at Rocks.* Walker LB, 1984. (K-3)

# Volcanic Action

**Purpose:** Simulating the discharge of built-up pressure below the earth's surface. Volcanic eruption is but one form of energy released from the earth.

**Materials:**

- 4 cups (1,000 mL) of flour
- 1 cup (250 mL) of salt
- 1.5 cups (375 mL) of warm water
- red food coloring*
- water
- vinegar
- baking soda
- newspaper
- pie tin or plate
- large bowl
- three 8 oz. (250 mL) paper cups*
- brown tempera paint*
- paint brush*
- student activity sheet*

**Procedure:**

1. In a large bowl, place 4 cups (1,000 mL) of flour and 1 cup (250 mL) of salt. Add to this 1.5 cups (375 mL) of warm water and carefully mix together using your hands.
2. When this mixture becomes a doughy substance, place it on a hard surface and knead it until it is smooth and rubbery.
3. Using the dough, mold it into a volcano, making sure to leave an opening at the top of the cone deep enough to conceal a paper cup. Bake in the oven for 30 minutes at 300° F (154° C).
4. Remove your volcano from the oven and allow it to cool. Place a paper cup inside the opening. Paint your volcano with brown tempera paint. Allow time for drying.
5. Place your model volcano on top of some newspaper and prepare it for a simulated eruption.
6. In a paper cup, mix 3 tbs. (45 mL) of baking soda with 4 oz. (118 mL) of water. Add red food coloring until this mixture turns red and pour it into the cup at the top of your volcano.
7. Pour 1 tsp. (5 mL) of vinegar into the red mixture and observe what happens.
8. Complete the attached activity sheet and return it and any unused school supplies on the date due.

**Why:** When you combine baking soda and vinegar, a chemical reaction is created that causes the liquid in your volcano to erupt. This reaction is similar to the eruption of a real volcano. When pressure from heat, steam, and movement below the earth's surface reaches an extreme, lava will erupt from the top of a volcano.

# Volcanic Action (cont.)

**Date Due:**_____

**Directions:** Draw a picture and then explain in your own words what you observed during your investigation.

_____

_____

_____

_____

_____

_____

**Student's Name:**_____

**Parent's Signature:**_____

38

# Volcanic Action (cont.)

## Introduction and Follow-up Activities

### Setting the Stage

- Discuss with students how and why volcanoes are formed.

- Have students look up the following terms: *crater, crust, lava, magma, magma chamber,* and *side vent.*

- Tell students that most of the world's volcanoes are found along the Ring of Fire, which encircles the Pacific Ocean.

- Pass out science kits and explain to students what they will be investigating at home.

### Extensions

- Review with students the results of their home investigations.

- Have students create a class model of an active and dormant volcano.

- Have students choose an active volcano anywhere in the world, research it, and give an oral report to the class.

### Closure

In a journal, have students draw a picture of a volcano and label the parts they studied.

### Related References

Barrett, Norman. *Volcanoes.* Watts LB, 1990. (3-5)

Branley, Franklyn M. *Volcanoes.* Harper LB, 1990. (3-4)

Challand, Helen J. *Volcanoes.* Children's LB, 1983. (1-4)

George, Michael. *Volcanoes.* Creative Ed. LB, 1991. (3-8)

Knapp, Brian. *Volcano.* Raintree LB, 1989. (3-6)

Simon, Seymour. *Volcanoes.* Morrow LB, 1988. (1-3)

# Developing Crystals to Eat

**Date Due:** _____

**Directions:** Draw a picture and then explain in your own words what happened during your investigation.

Student's Name: _____

Parent's Signature: _____

✂ - - - - - - - - - - - - - - - - - - - - - - - - - - - - - - - - - - - - - -

# Developing Crystals to Eat

**Purpose:** To better understand the formation of crystals.

**Materials:**
- medium size sauce pan
- measuring cups
- four craft sticks*
- water
- food coloring (optional)*
- stirring spoon (wooden)
- four small glasses
- sugar
- student activity sheet*
- magnifying lens*

**Procedure:**

1. In a medium saucepan combine 4 1/2 cups (1 L) of water and 2 cups (500 g) of sugar. The sugar may not all dissolve immediately.

2. Heat your solution until it comes to a boil, stirring occasionally. Continue to let it boil for two minutes.

3. Before pouring your solution into the four glasses, make sure the glasses are warm.

4. Pour a quarter of the solution into each glass, add food coloring if desired, and stir with a craft stick.

5. Leave a craft stick in each solution, place in a well-lit area, and let stand for about a week.

6. Observe at least once a day while the crystals are developing.

7. At the end of the week, examine your crystals with a magnifying lens and then taste what has developed.

8. Complete the attached activity sheet and return it and any unused school supplies on the date due.

**Why:** When you heated the water, the sugar crystals dissolved, thereby creating a supersaturated solution. As the water cools and evaporates, the sugar crystals will re-form along the craftstick.

# Developing Crystals to Eat (cont.)

## Introduction and Follow-up Activities

### Setting the Stage

- Have students brainstorm a list of crystals. Make a master list for your class.

- See if students can give some of the uses for the crystals on the master list.

- Ask students how they think crystals are formed.

### Extensions

- Pass out science kits and explain to students what they will be investigating at home.

- Have students repeat this activity using different substances (e.g., salt, alum, etc.).

- Put on display as many different crystals as you can find, either real or pictures.

### Closure

In a journal, have students write a story about finding a magic crystal.

### Related References

Bell, Robert A. *Crystals.* Western Pub., 1992. (K-5)

Podendorf, Illa. *Rocks & Minerals.* Children's LB, 1982. (1-4)

Selsam, Millicent E. and Joyce Hunt. *A First Look at Rocks.* Walker LB, 1984. (K-3)

Stang, Jean. *Crystals & Crystal Gardens You Can Grow.* Watts, 1990. (PS-3)

# Modeling the Earth

**Date Due:** _____

**Directions:** Draw a picture and then explain in your own words what happened during your investigation.

Student's Name: _____

Parent's Signature: _____

---

# Modeling the Earth

**Purpose:** To build a handheld model of the earth, in order to see the different layers that exist.

**Materials:**

- aluminum foil
- string*
- modeling clay (red, green, blue, and brown)*
- diagram of earth's layers*
- student activity sheet*

**Procedure:**

1. Take a piece of aluminum foil and roll it into a ball about the size of a marble. This will be the inner core of your earth model. Use the diagram of the earth's layers as reference.

2. Cover the foil using the red clay, so it is about .25" (.64 cm) thick. This will be the outer core of your earth model.

3. Cover the red clay with green clay, so it is about .75" (1.8 cm) thick. This will be the mantle of your earth model.

4. Cover the green clay with blue clay, just thick enough so the mantle does not show through. This is the crust of the earth, although the blue represents the oceans of the world.

5. Using the brown clay, make the seven continents around the world. Your earth model is complete.

6. In order to see the different layers you have created, take a piece of string and wrap it around the center of your model. Pull the strings gradually as they cut your model in half. When you have reached the foil, stop! Remove the string and slowly pull apart your model. You can now observe the inside of the earth.

7. Complete the attached activity sheet and return it and any unused school supplies on the date due.

©1995 Teacher Created Materials, Inc.

# Modeling the Earth (cont.)

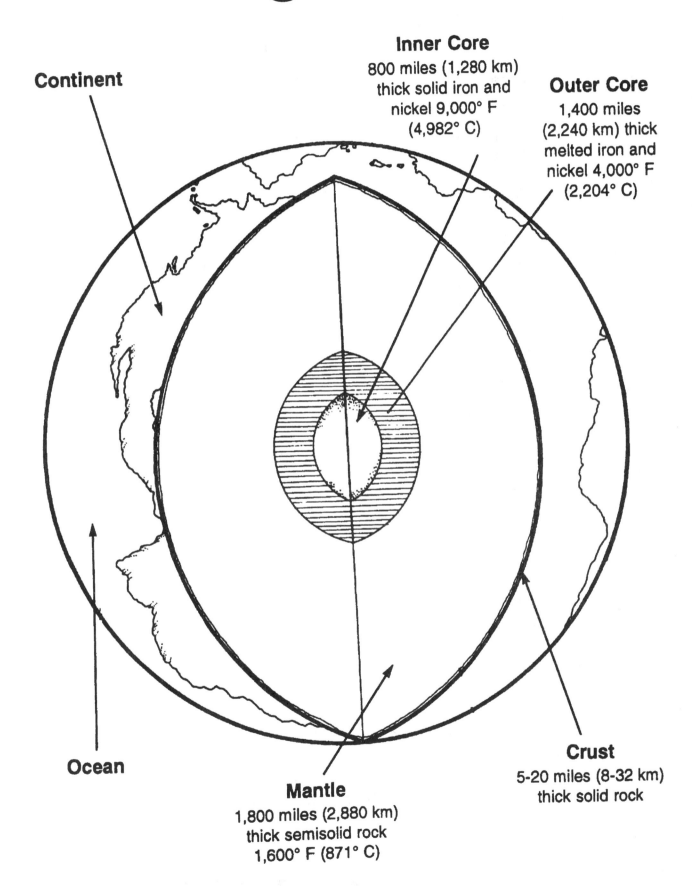

**Continent**

**Inner Core**
800 miles (1,280 km) thick solid iron and nickel 9,000° F (4,982° C)

**Outer Core**
1,400 miles (2,240 km) thick melted iron and nickel 4,000° F (2,204° C)

**Ocean**

**Mantle**
1,800 miles (2,880 km) thick semisolid rock 1,600° F (871° C)

**Crust**
5-20 miles (8-32 km) thick solid rock

# Modeling the Earth (cont.)

## Introduction and Follow-up Activities

### Setting the Stage

- See if students know how many layers of the earth there are.

- After students have made their guesses, tell them how many layers and what they are.

- Discuss what the earth is made of and how scientists think the earth came to be.

- Have students answer the question "Why is it important to know what the earth is made of?"

- Pass out science kits and explain to students what they will be investigating at home.

### Extensions

- Review with students the results of their home investigations.

- Have students list the layers of the earth and tell what each layer is made of.

- Have students share their models of the earth with the rest of the class.

- Have students pick something about the earth they are interested in, research it, and then give an oral report about what they found out.

### Closure

In a journal, have students write a story about a journey to the center of the earth.

### Related References

Branley, Franklyn M. *What Makes Day and Night.* Harper LB, 1986. (1-3)

Cole, Joanna. *The Magic School Bus Inside the Earth.* Scholastic, 1987. (2-5)

Lowery, Linda. *Earth Day.* Carolrhoda, 1991. (2-3)

McNulty, Faith. *How to Dig a Hole to the Other Side of the World.* Harper LB, 1979. (2-4)

Murray, Peter. *Planet Earth.* Child's World LB, 1993. (2-4)

Savan, Beth. *Earthwatch: Earthcycles and Ecosystems.* Addison Wesley LB, 1992. (3-7)

# Nature's Oven

**Purpose:** To construct a solar cooker from materials provided and then harness the sun's energy to cook an apple.

**Materials:**

- one piece of tagboard 12" x 18" (30 cm x 45 cm)*
- black construction paper*
- aluminum foil (enough to cover the tagboard)
- an apple
- plastic wrap
- scissors
- glue
- transparent tape
- toothpick*
- large paper cup*
- student activity sheet*

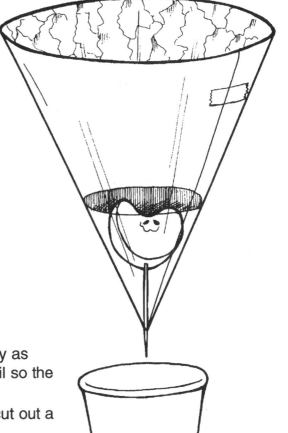

**Procedure:**

1. Glue a piece of aluminum foil as smoothly as possible to the tagboard. Use enough foil so the tagboard is completely covered.
2. Once the foil has dried to the tagboard, cut out a large circle.
3. From your piece of black construction paper, cut a circle with a 2-3" (5-7.5 cm) diameter, glue it to the center of your foil circle, and allow time for the glue to dry.
4. Cut a line from the outside of your foil circle to the center, shape it into a cone, and then tape it in place.
5. Push a toothpick through the center of your cone. Attach an apple slice to the top of the toothpick so the apple is inside the cone and then cover the top of the cone with a piece of plastic wrap.
6. Place your cone inside a paper cup to stabilize it, and then place your solar cooker in the sun to cook your apple.
7. When your apple has been cooked to your desire, enjoy a healthy snack from the sun.
8. Complete the attached activity sheet and return it and any unused school supplies on the date due.

**Why:** The foil reflects the sun's rays onto the black construction paper, which then heats the apple. The apple is able to cook because the plastic wrap traps in the sun's heat that has been captured.

# Nature's Oven (cont.)

**Date Due:**_____

**Directions:** Draw a picture and then explain in your own words what you observed during your investigation.

_____

_____

_____

_____

_____

_____

Student's Name: _____

Parent's Signature: _____

# Nature's Oven (cont.)

## Introduction and Follow-up Activities

### Setting the Stage

- Have a class discussion about solar energy.

- Ask your students how solar energy is used.

- Ask your students if any of them have solar powered devices in their families' homes.

- Pass out science kits and explain to students what they will be investigating at home.

### Extensions

- Review with students the results of their home investigations.

- Have students design another type of solar cooker using different materials. (e.g., boxes, clear plastic, glass, etc.)

- Have students research the history of solar energy.

### Closure

In a journal, have students write down their thoughts and feelings if their only heat source came from the sun.

### Related References

Baker, Susan. *First Look at Using Energy.* Stevens LB, 1991. (1-2)

Branley, Franklyn M. *The Sun: Our Nearest Star.* Harper LB, 1988. (1-3)

Cobb, Vicki. *Why Doesn't the Sun Burn Out? And Other Not Such Dumb Questions About Energy.* Dutton, 1990. (2-5)

Levine, Shar & Allison Grafton. *Projects for a Healthy Planet: Simple Environmental Experiments for Kids.* Wiley LB, 1992. (3-7)

Simon, Seymour. *The Sun.* Morrow LB, 1986. (3-5)

# What's in a Cloud?

**Date Due:** _____

**Directions:** Draw a picture and then explain in your own words what happened during your investigation.

Student's Name: _____

Parent's Signature: _____

---

# What's in a Cloud?

**Purpose:** To understand how clouds form and what is inside them.

**Materials:**

- two small clear plastic cups*
- hot water
- flashlight (optional)
- magnifying lens*
- student activity sheet*

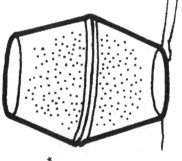

**Procedure:**

1. Fill one of your plastic cups 1/3 full of hot water.

2. Take the second plastic cup and place it upside down on the first cup. Make sure the rims meet evenly and the cups are sealed.

3. Observe what is happening in the cups. Turn the lights out and use a flashlight to observe your cloud. You may also get a better view using a magnifying lens.

4. Complete the attached activity sheet and return it and any unused school supplies on the date due.

**Why:** A cloud contains billions of tiny water or ice droplets that form around dust or salt. Clouds form when water vapor (a gas) changes into liquid and warm and cold air meet. In the activity, the warm, moisture-saturated air in the bottom of the cup moved upward and met the cooler air at the top of the cup.

48

# What's in a Cloud? (cont.)

## Introduction and Follow-up Activities

### Setting the Stage

- Review with students the three states of water—solid, liquid, and gas.

- Ask students if they know where clouds come from.

- Ask students if they have ever made a cloud. Then tell them if they have seen their breath, they have made a cloud.

- Pass out science kits and explain to students what they will be investigating at home.

### Extensions

- Review with students the results of their home investigations.

- Have students learn about all of the different types of clouds that exist.

- Have students create classroom clouds out of materials you provide them in class.

### Closure

On a day when there are a lot of clouds in the sky, take students outside, have them lie down in the grass, and watch as the clouds pass over their heads. Have students call out shapes as they see them.

### Related References

Ardley, Neil. *The Science Book of Weather.* Harcourt, 1992. (3-6)

dePaola, Tomie. *The Cloud Book*. Holiday LB, 1975. (K-3)

Fowler, Allan. *What's the Weather Today?* Children's LB, 1991. (1-3)

Gibbons, Gail. *Weather Forecasting.* Macmillan, 1987. (K-3)

Goldsen, Louise. *Weather.* Scholastic, 1991. (K-2)

Greene, Carol. *Hi, Clouds.* Children's LB, 1983. (K-2)

Lambert, David. *Weather.* Troll LB, 1990. (3-5)

Ray, Deborah Kogan. *The Cloud.* Harper Collins, 1984. (all)

Stacey, Tom. *Earth, Sea, and Sky.* Random Paper, 1991. (2-6)

# Weight: Earth vs. Other Planets

**Date Due:** _____

**Directions:** Explain in your own words what happened during your investigation.

_____

_____

_____

_____

_____

_____

_____

_____

**Student's Name:** _____

**Parent's Signature:** _____

&#9986;

# Weight: Earth vs. Other Planets

**Purpose:** To calculate your weight as it would be on the moon and all the other planets in our solar system.

**Materials:**

- calculator
- scale
- student activity sheets*

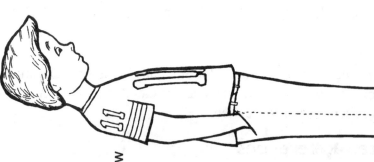

**Procedure:**

1. Get on a scale to determine how much you weigh.

2. On your student activity sheet, fill in your weight in the appropriate column, then calculate your weight on the moon and the other plants in the solar system.

3. Once you have calculated your weights for all of the different planets, construct a line graph on the activity sheet provided.

4. Complete the attached activity sheets and return them and any unused school supplies on the date due.

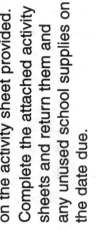

# Weight: Earth vs. Other Planets (cont.)

**Directions:** Fill in your weight in the correct column and calculate what your weight would be on the moon and the other planets in our solar system.

| Planet | Surface Gravity | | Your Weight on Earth | New Weight |
|--------|-----------------|---|----------------------|------------|
| Mercury | .38 | x | | |
| Venus | .90 | x | | |
| Earth | 1.00 | x | | |
| Mars | .38 | x | | |
| Jupiter | 2.64 | x | | |
| Saturn | 1.13 | x | | |
| Uranus | .89 | x | | |
| Neptune | 1.13 | x | | |
| Pluto | .06 | x | | |
| Earth's Moon | .17 | x | | |

# Weight: Earth vs. Other Planets (cont.)

**Directions:** Chart your weight calculations from the different planets, using a line graph.

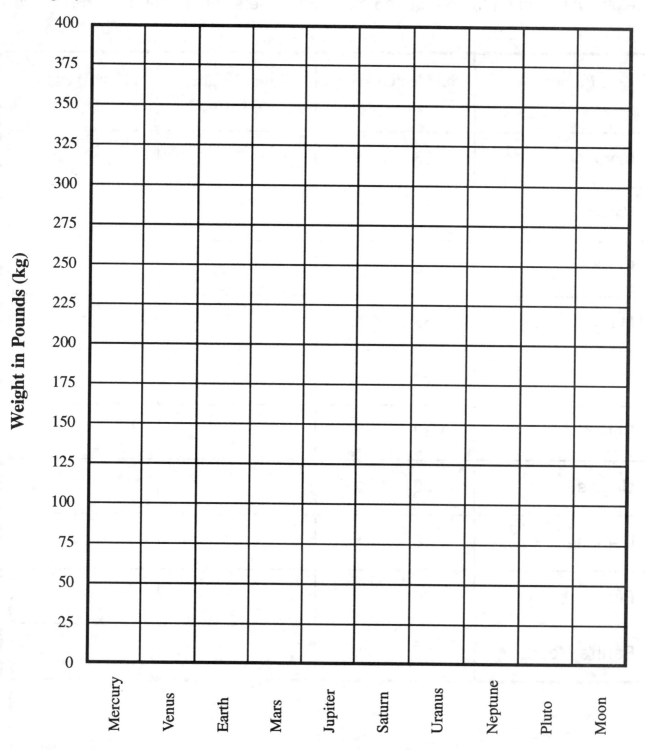

**Location**

# Weight: Earth vs. Other Planets (cont.)

## Introduction and Follow-up Activities

### Setting the Stage

- Ask students to name all of the planets in our solar system. Fill in any planets they may leave out.

- Discuss with students the concepts of mass and gravity and how the two are related.

- Explain to students that the planets and the moon vary in mass as well as size and that the greater the mass, the more gravitational pull. This means you weigh more on a planet or moon having more mass than the Earth and less on those having less mass than Earth.

- Pass out activity sheets and explain to students what they will be investigating at home.

### Extensions

- Review with students the results of their home investigations.

- Make a master graph of your class, showing their weight on all the different planets and the moon.

- Plan a visit for your class to a local planetarium.

### Closure

In a journal, have students write and illustrate a story describing what it would feel like to walk on another planet.

### Related References

Bendick, Jeanne. *The Planets: Neighbors in Space.* Millbrook LB, 1991. (2-4)

Branley, Franklyn M. *The Planets in Our Solar System.* Harper LB, 1987. (2-4)

Fowler, Allan. *The Sun's Family of Planets.* Children's LB, 1992. (1-2)

Jones, Brian. *Space: A Three-Dimensional Journey.* Dial, 1991. (1-4)

Simon, Seymour. *Our Solar System.* Morrow LB, 1992. (2-6)

# Balloon Racers

**Date Due:** _____

**Directions:** Draw a picture and then explain in your own words what happened during your investigation.

Student's Name: _____

Parent's Signature: _____

---

# Balloon Racers

**Purpose:** To observe Newton's Third Law of Motion—for every action there is an equal and opposite reaction.

**Materials:**

- one hot-dog shaped balloon*
- 3 yds. (2.7 m) of string*
- masking tape*
- meter or yard stick
- student activity sheet*

**Procedure:**

1. Attach one end of the string waist high to an object that will not move.

2. Feed the free end of the string through the straw.

3. Attach three pieces of masking tape to the straw—one across the left side, one across the middle, and one across the right side.

4. Inflate your balloon, pinch the end closed, and attach it to the straw so the open end of your balloon faces the side of the string not tied.

5. Hold the loose end of the string tight, move your balloon to the end of the string you are holding, and release.

6. Observe what happens and measure the distance your balloon travels. Repeat this investigation several times. On the student activity sheet provided, record the distances your balloon travels.

7. Complete the attached activity sheet and return it and any unused school supplies on the date due.

**Why:** When the air was released from the back of the balloon racer, it pushed the balloon forward, illustrating Newton's Second Law of Motion.

# Balloon Racers (cont.)

## Introduction and Follow-up Activities

### Setting the Stage

- Show students a video of the space shuttle taking off.

- Explain to students that forces work in pairs that are equal and opposite. The key idea is that they do not act on the same thing. If they did, nothing would move, because all forces would cancel and always remain balanced. The rocket casing provides a force, or pressure, on the fuel. The burning fuel provides an equal and opposite force on the rocket. The first force acts to expel the fuel; the second force acts to move the rocket.

- Pass out science kits and explain to students what they will be investigating at home.

### Extensions

- Review with students the results of their home investigations.

- Have students repeat their investigations, this time using different shaped balloons, more weight, and a different angle for the string.

- As a class project, have students build model rockets and then have a launching party at some future date.

### Closure

In a journal, have students write a story about flying to the moon.

### Related References

Abernathy, Susan. *Space Machines.* Western Publishing Co., 1991. (all)

Branley, Franklyn. *Rockets & Satellites.* Harper Paper, 1987. (2-4)

Darling, David J. *Could You Ever Fly to the Stars?* Macmillan LB, 1991. (3-6)

Evans, David & Claudette Williams. *Make It Change.* Darling, 1992. (1-4)

Murphy, Brian. *Experiment with Movement.* Lerner LB, (2-4)

Stille, Darlene K. *Spacecraft.* Children's LB, 1991. (1-3)

# Straw Strength

**Purpose:** To observe how much weight one drinking straw can hold. (Then repeat the same activity with several straws.)

**Materials:**

- a 16 oz (500 mL) plastic cup*
- six drinking straws*
- two pieces of string 18" (45 cm) and 12" (30 cm)*
- two small rubber bands*
- scissors
- measuring cup
- large sauce pan
- water
- student activity sheet*

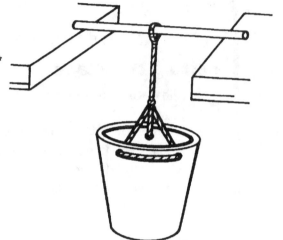

**Procedure:**

1. Using a pair of scissors, poke three holes equally spaced around the rim of your plastic cup.

2. Wrap the shorter string around the rim of your cup once and cut off the excess string.

3. Thread the ends of the string through two of the holes in your cup and tie the ends together to make a loop.

4. Take the second piece of string, thread it through the third hole, tie it off, and then tie it to the loop so the cup will hang level.

5. Tie a loop in the free end of the string and thread a straw through the loop. Then, suspend the straw between two chairs or tables, with the cup hanging in the middle.

6. Slowly add water to the hanging cup; keep pouring water until the straw buckles. Catch the cup before it hits the ground and measure how much water was in the cup, using your measuring cup. Make sure the sauce pan is below your work area to catch any water spillage.

7. Repeat this activity several times, each time adding an additional straw. Observe the differences. Note: When you use three or more straws, rubber band the ends together.

8. Complete the attached activity sheet and return it and any unused school supplies on the date due.

**Why:** A flat piece of material is not very strong, but roll it into a tube and it can withstand a great deal of weight. This is because of the shape that is created within each half cylinder. This shape distributes the force pushing down, as well as pushing up.

# Straw Strength (cont.)

**Date Due:**_____

**Directions:** Draw a picture and then explain in your own words what you observed during your investigation.

_____

_____

_____

_____

_____

_____

Student's Name: _____

Parent's Signature: _____

# Straw Strength (cont.)

## Introduction and Follow-up Activities

### Setting the Stage

- Have a class discussion about weight (e.g., What is it?, Why does it occur?, How is it used?, etc.).

- Ask students how much weight a piece of paper might be able to hold.

- Show your students the strength or weakness of an ordinary piece of paper.

- Demonstration:  Place a sheet of paper between two chairs and then place a cup in the middle of the paper.  Have students observe what happens.  Then make an accordion fold of the paper, place it between the chairs, and place the same cup in the middle of the paper.  Have students observe what happens.  Note any differences.

- Pass out science kits and explain to students what they will be investigating at home.

### Extensions

- Review with students the results of their home investigations.

- Have a class contest seeing whose bridge can hold the most weight.

- Invite a speaker to class that can lead a discussion on structural strength.  Allow students to ask questions.

### Closure

In a journal, have students design a unique bridge using materials of their own choosing.

### Related References

Ardley, Neil. *The Science Book of Gravity.*  Harcourt, 1992. (3-6)

Branley, Franklyn M. *Gravity Is a Mystery.*  HarpC Child Bks., 1986. (PS-3)

Evans, David & Claudette Williams. *Make It Change.*  Dorling, 1992. (1-4)

Simon, Seymour. *Soap Bubble Magic.*  Lothrop LB, 1985. (K-3)

Wildsmith, Brian. *What the Moon Saw.*  Oxford Univ. Press, 1978. (PS-1)

# Steam Power

**Date Due:** _____

**Directions:** Draw a picture and then explain in your own words what happened during your investigation.

Student's Name: _____

Parent's Signature: _____

---

# Steam Power

**Purpose:** To create enough steam power to make a model boat move through the water.

**Materials:**

- a medium sized candle*
- modeling clay*
- a test tube or a hollow metal tube (e.g., cigar holder, indigestion tablets holder, etc.)*
- test tube stopper with a small tubing hole*
- a clean sardine can
- matches
- knife
- water
- student activity sheet*

**Procedure:**

1. Cut your candle into three small pieces and fit them inside the sardine can. Each piece needs to have a wick.

2. Make a small hole in the cap of the metal tube. Fill the tube with about an 1" (2.5 cm) of water and then screw on the cap. Or use the glass test tube with the stopper instead.

3. Place the tube over the candles, and using the modeling clay, secure the tube to the top edges of the sardine can.

4. Place your boat in a large tub of water, light the candles, and observe what happens.

5. Complete the attached activity sheet and return it with any unused school supplies on the date due.

**Why:** As the candles heat the water, steam is eventually produced. When the steam escapes through the small hole in the cap, it will cause the boat to move forward.

# Steam Power (cont.)

## Introduction and Follow-up Activities

### Setting the Stage

- Have students list as many different types of engines as they think exist.

- Combine your students individual lists into a master list for the class. Then have them try to figure out the use of each engine listed. Fill in the engine uses they do not know.

- Ask students if they can think of a specific use for a steam powered engine. Model the construction of a sardine-can steamboat.

- Pass out science kits and explain to students what they will be investigating at home.

### Extensions

- Review with students the results of their home investigations.

- Have students research the steam engine (i.e., who developed it, when, what were its uses, etc.).

- Have students give oral reports of their research.

### Closure

In a journal, have students design a steam engine different than the one they made.

### Related References

Ardley, Neil. *The Science Book of Motion.* Harcourt, 1992. (3-6)

Baker, Susan. *First Look At Using Energy.* Stevens LB, 1991. (1-2)

Cobb, Vicki. *Why Doesn't the Earth Fall Up? And Other Not Such Dumb Questions About Motion.* Dutton, 1989. (2-4)

Evans, David & Claudette Williams. *Make It Change.* Darling, 1992. (1-4)

Murphy, Brian. *Experiment with Movement.* Lerner LB, (2-4)

Taylor, Kim. *Action.* Wiley, 1992. (3-5)

# Mysterious Goop

**Date Due:** _____

**Directions:** Draw a picture and then explain in your own words what you observed during your investigation.

[ drawing box ]

_____

_____

_____

_____

_____

_____

_____

**Student's Name:** _____

**Parent's Signature:** _____

# Mysterious Goop

**Purpose:** To observe *suspension* and *separation*.

**Materials:**

- cornstarch*
- food coloring (any color)*
- water
- large bowl
- measuring cups
- mixing spoon
- student activity sheet*

**Procedure:**

1. Pour 2 cups (500 mL) of cornstarch into a large mixing bowl.

2. Add to that 1 cup (250 mL) of water and mix together with mixing spoon.

3. While mixing together the cornstarch and water, add food coloring until you get the color you desire.

4. When you have finished mixing together the mysterious goop, you may begin to examine the mixture.

5. Complete the attached activity sheet and return it and any school supplies on the date due.

**Why:** By mixing cornstarch and water you have created "suspension." This condition occurs when the particles of a substance (cornstarch) slowly separate from a liquid (water). When you squeeze the suspended mixture together it feels like a solid. When you allow the suspended mixture to stand on its own, the liquid and solid parts will separate, making it feel like a liquid. This reaction is similar to that of sandy or muddy water.

# Mysterious Goop (cont.)

## Introduction and Follow-up Activities

### Setting the Stage

- Have students define the terms *mixture* and *solution.*

- Once students are familiar with the above terms, give them a list of mixtures and solutions and see if they can categorize them properly.

- Pass out science kits and explain to students what they will be investigating at home.

### Extensions

- Review with students the results of their home investigations.

- Have students think about the surface of a planet being covered with a mixture similar to our mysterious goop. What might be some of the possible modes of transportation for mobility on this planet?

- Have students think about the earth. Is there any surface on the earth that resembles the mysterious goop mixture?

### Closure

In a journal, have students design a vehicle that can drive on top of the mysterious goop.

### Related References

Challand, Helen J. *Experiments with Chemistry.* Children's, 1988. (all)

Cobb, Vicki. *Why Can't You Unscramble an Egg? And Other Not Such Dumb Questions About Matter.* Dutton, 1993. (3-6)

Cooper, Christopher. *Matter.* Dorling LB, 1992. (all)

Evans, David & Claudette Williams. *Make It Change.* Darling, 1992. (1-4)

Whyman, Kathryn. *Chemical Changes.* Watts, 1986. (all)

# Magical Glob

**Date Due:** _____

**Directions:** Draw a picture and then explain in your own words what happened during your investigation.

Student's Name: _____

Parent's Signature: _____

✂

# Magical Glob

**Purpose:** To demonstrate how certain simple compounds create polymers.

**Materials:**

- white glue*
- plastic sealable bag*
- measuring cup
- food coloring (optional)
- borax solution*
- two spoons
- water
- student activity sheet*

**Procedure:** *(Teacher Instructions)*

1. Combine 1/2 cup (125 g) of borax with 1 qt (1 L) of warm tap water.

2. Each student will need at least 2 tsp (10 mL) of the borax solution.

**Procedure:** *(Student Instructions)*

1. In your plastic bag combine 2-3 tsps (10-15 mL) of water with 1 tbs (15 mL) of glue. Seal the bag and mix the glue and water by squishing the bag.

2. Now add 2 tsps (10 mL) of the borax solution. Reseal the bag, making sure there is no air inside. Mix the solution the same as above.

3. When the mixture shows signs of bonding together, remove it from the bag and roll in the palms of your hands until you have reached a desired consistency.

4. Complete the attached activity sheet and return it and any unused school supplies on the date due.

**Why:** You have created a polymer. The active ingredient in white glue is polyvinyl acetate. When this ingredient is combined with borax, a bond is created forming the magical glob.

# Magical Glob (cont.)

## Introduction and Follow-up Activities

### Setting the Stage

- Define and possibly illustrate for your students the terms *polymer* and *monomer.*

- Once students have an understanding of what the terms mean, discuss some of the uses of polymers.

- Ask students if they think polymers are used in their homes.

- Pass out science kits and explain to students what they will be investigating at home.

### Extensions

- Review with students the results of their home investigations.

- Bring in some examples of polymers for students to see.

- Have a class discussion about the kinds of things polymers might be used for in the future.

### Closure

In a journal, have students create a polymer, draw a picture of what it might look like, and explain how it could be used.

### Related References

Challand, Helen J. *Experiments with Chemistry.* Children's, 1988. (all)

Cobb, Vicki. *Why Can't You Unscramble an Egg? And Other Not Such Dumb Questions About Matter.* Dutton, 1993. (3-6)

Cooper, Christopher. *Matter.* Dorling LB, 1992. (all)

Evans, David & Claudette Williams. *Make It Change.* Darling, 1992. (1-4)

Whyman, Kathryn. *Chemical Changes.* Watts, 1986. (all)

# Fire Stopper

**Date Due:** _____

**Directions:** Draw a picture and then explain in your own words what happened during your investigation.

Student's Name: _____

Parent's Signature: _____

✂

# Fire Stopper

**Purpose:** Creating a chemical change in order to put out a flame.

**Materials:**
- candle*
- small glass jar
- vinegar
- baking soda
- matches
- tablespoon
- measuring cup
- student activity sheet*

**Procedure:**

1. Place your candle on a plate or in a bowl standing up.

2. Combine in the glass jar 1 tbs (15 g) of baking soda with 3-4 oz (90-120 mL) of vinegar.

3. As the bubbles begin to form, hold the jar over the lit candle, tipping the jar as if you were pouring out its contents, but do **not** pour out the mixture.

4. Observe what happens to the flame and give your best explanation.

5. Complete the attached activity sheet and return it and any unused school supplies on the date due.

**Why:** When baking soda and vinegar are combined, the reaction creates carbon dioxide. Carbon dioxide is lighter than the mixture and the air already in the jar, but it is heavier than the atmosphere outside the jar. So when you tip the jar over, the carbon dioxide will pour out and extinguish the flame.

# Fire Stopper (cont.)

## Introduction and Follow-up Activities

### Setting the Stage

- Have students define the term *chemical change*.

- Discuss with students different ways a chemical change can be detected.

- After students understand what a chemical change is and how it can be detected, have them give examples of chemical changes.

- Pass out science kits and explain to students what they will be investigating at home.

### Extensions

- Review with students the results of their home investigations.

- Have students repeat the activity, this time trying to put out a larger flame.

- Have students perform other activities involving chemical reactions.

### Closure

In a journal, draw a picture of what you think the chemical reaction taking place looks like.

### Related References

Challand, Helen J. *Experiments with Chemistry.* Children's, 1988. (all)

Cobb, Vicki. *Why Can't You Unscramble an Egg? And Other Not Such Dumb Questions About Matter.* Dutton, 1993. (3-6)

Cooper, Christopher. *Matter.* Dorling LB, 1992. (all)

Evans, David & Claudette Williams. *Make It Change.* Darling, 1992. (1-4)

Whyman, Kathryn. *Chemical Changes.* Watts, 1986. (all)

# Static Electricity

**Date Due:** _____

**Directions:** Draw a picture and then explain in your own words what happened during your investigation.

Student's Name: _____

Parent's Signature: _____

# Static Electricity

**Purpose:** To create static charges from a variety of materials.

**Materials:**
- two balloons*
- Rice Krispies®*
- paper plate*
- wool cloth*
- salt and pepper
- student activity sheet*

**Procedure:**

1. Inflate one balloon, knot it, rub it on your head or with a wool cloth, and try to stick it on a wall. Observe what happens.

2. On your paper plate make a combined pile of salt and pepper. Then, rub the already inflated balloon with the wool cloth and place it just above the salt and pepper. Observe what happens.

3. Put 6-12 Rice Krispies® inside the second balloon, inflate it, and knot it. Then, rub it with the wool cloth, touch one of your fingers to the balloon where the Rice Krispies® are, and observe what happens.

4. Complete the attached activity sheet and return it with any unused school supplies on the date due.

**Why:** Rubbing the balloon on your head or with a wool cloth creates a negative charge. The wall which has a positive charge attracts the negatively charged balloon, allowing the balloon to stick to the wall. The same thing occurs with the balloon and the pepper. The Rice Krispies® jump inside the balloon because the balloon has been given a negative charge from the wool cloth. As your finger approaches the balloon it picks up a positive charge through magnetic induction just like the Rice Krispies® and the two like charges repel each other.

# Static Electricity (cont.)

## Introduction and Follow-up Activities

### Setting the Stage

- Have students take turns telling what they know about static electricity.

- Ask students if they have ever been shocked while flipping on a light switch. Have them try to explain what happened.

- After students have explained and shared what they know about static electricity, fill in the missing blanks.

- Pass out science kits and explain to students what they will be investigating at home.

### Extensions

- Review with students the results of their home investigations.

- Have students repeat this experience in a variety of weather conditions.

- Have students research the history of static electricity and find out its origin.

- Allow students to share their new information with the class.

### Closure

In a journal, have students explain static electricity.

### Related References

Ardley, Neil. *The Science Book of Electricity.* HBJ, 1991. (3-6)

Bailey, Mark W. *Electricity.* Raintree LB, 1988. (all)

Bains, Rae. *Discovering Electricity.* Troll LB, 1982. (1-3)

Berger, Melvin. *Switch On, Switch Off.* Harper LB, 1989. (K-3)

Hoban, Russell. *Arthur's New Power.* Harper LB, 1978. (2-3)

Markle, Sandra. *Power Up: Experiments, Puzzles, and Games Exploring Electricity.* Macmillan, 1989. (3-5)

Taylor, Barbara. *Electricity & Magnets.* Watts LB, 1990. (3-6)

# Short-Circuited

**Date Due:** _____

**Directions:** Draw a picture and then explain in your own words what happened during your investigation.

Student's Name: _____

Parent's Signature: _____

# Short-Circuited

**Purpose:** To observe what happens when a bare wire is placed in the path of a resistor (light bulb).

**Materials:**
- a 1.5 volt ("D") battery*
- three pieces of insulated copper wire, 12" (30 cm) long with the ends exposed*
- a 1.5 volt bulb and holder*
- craft knife*
- transparent tape
- student activity sheet*

**Procedure:** *(To be done at school.)*
1. Give each student three pieces of insulated wire.
2. Using a craft knife, strip off a 1" (2.5 cm) strip of insulation in the middle of two pieces of wire.

**Procedure:** *(To be done at home.)*
1. Attach an exposed end from each wire to the two ends of the bulb holder. Note: If you do not have a bulb holder, hold one wire to the metal side of the bulb base and the other wire to the bottom of the bulb.
2. Take the other ends of the wires and tape them to the top and bottom of your battery. Observe what happens.
3. Place the exposed ends of the third wire on top of the exposed areas of the wires attached to the bulb. Observe what happens.
4. Complete the attached activity sheet and return it and any unused school supplies on the date due.

**Why:** When the third wire is placed into the circuit, the light goes out. This is because electricity will follow the shortest and easiest way back to its power source. Electricity follows the path of least resistance.

# Short-Circuited (cont.)

## Introduction and Follow-up Activities

### Setting the Stage

- Ask students to raise their hands if they have been in the house when the lights have gone out. Ask them why they think it happens.

- Have students define the terms *electric current* and *circuit*.

- Discuss with students that in order for electricity to accomplish meaningful work, it must flow through a circuit.

- Pass out science kits and explain to students what they will be investigating at home.

### Extensions

- Review with students the results of their home investigations.

- See if students can repair a circuit once it has been short-circuited.

- Have students make a list of things that can happen if a piece of electrical equipment short-circuits.

- Have students brainstorm some ideas of how to prevent short circuits from happening.

### Closure

In a journal, have students draw a picture of something short-circuiting and then how to prevent the short circuit from occurring.

### Related References

Ardley, Neil. *The Science Book of Electricity.* HBJ, 1991. (3-6)

Bailey, Mark W. *Electricity.* Raintree LB, 1988. (all)

Bains, Rae. *Discovering Electricity.* Troll LB, 1982. (1-3)

Berger, Melvin. *Switch On, Switch Off.* Harper LB, 1989. (K-3)

Hoban, Russell. *Arthur's New Power.* Harper LB, 1978. (2-3)

Markle, Sandra. *Power Up: Experiments, Puzzles, and Games Exploring Electricity.* Macmillan, 1989. (3-5)

Taylor, Barbara. *Electricity & Magnets.* Watts LB, 1990. (3-6)

# Homemade Magnets

**Date Due:** _____

**Directions:** Draw a picture and then explain in your own words what you observed during your investigation.

[ ]

_____

_____

_____

_____

_____

Student's Name: _____

Parent's Signature: _____

# Homemade Magnets

**Purpose:** To turn a nail and then ordinary household products into temporary magnets.

**Materials:**

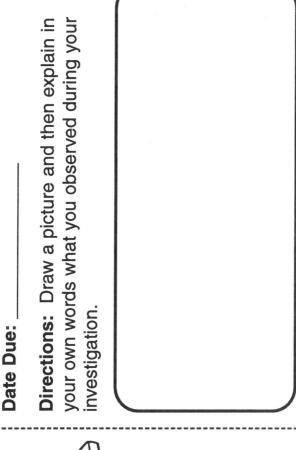

- large bar magnet*
- large nail*
- iron filings*
- miscellaneous items (coins, nails, nuts and bolts, paper clips, pencil, safety pins, etc.)
- student activity sheet*

**Procedure**

1. Using the large nail, try and pick up some of the iron filings. What happens?

2. Now, take the large bar magnet and stroke the nail 30 times in the same direction.

3. Try to pick up the iron filings with your new temporary magnet. What happens this time?

4. Once you are able to pick up the filings, see what other items you can pick up with the magnetized nail.

5. Complete the attached activity sheet and return it and any school supplies on the date due.

**Why:** In an ordinary piece of metal, the atoms that make it up already have magnetic domains that point in several different directions, neutralizing its magnetic field. In a magnetized piece of metal, the magnetic domains point in the same direction, creating a magnetic field. Some non-magnetic metals can be magnetized by aligning the magnetic domains in the same direction.

# Homemade Magnets (cont.)

## Introduction and Follow-up Activities

### Setting the Stage

- Display for students a variety of traditional magnets (i.e., bar, horseshoe, u-shaped, etc.)

- Discuss with students the reasons these objects are magnetic.

- Ask students if they think other objects might be able to act like a magnet. Make a master list for your class.

- Pass out science kits and explain to students what they will be investigating at home.

### Extensions

- Review with students the results of their home investigations.

- Have students time how long the nail will stay magnetized.

- Have students stroke the nail an additional 30 times. Ask them if this strengthens their magnetic nails to pick up more items, as well as causing them to remain magnetic for a longer period of time.

- Have students drop their magnetic nails on the ground and then try and pick something up. What happens?

### Closure

In a journal, have students draw a picture of a piece of metal with scattered atoms (non-magnetic) and a picture of a piece of metal with aligned atoms (magnetic).

### Related References

Ardley, Neil. *The Science Book of Magnets.* HBJ, 1991. (3-6)

Kirkpatrick, Rena K. *Look at Magnets.* Raintree LB, 1985. (K-2)

Taylor, Barbara. *Electricity & Magnets.* Watts LB, 1990. (3-6)

VanCleave Janice. *Magnets: Mind Boggling Experiments You Can Turn into Science Fair Projects.* Wiley Paper, 1993. (4-5)

# Sound Waves

**Date Due:** _____

**Directions:** Draw a picture and then explain in your own words what happened during your investigation.

Student's Name: _____

Parent's Signature: _____

---

# Sound Waves

**Purpose:** To follow the flow of sound waves between a person and an object.

**Materials:**
- a wire coat hanger
- two pieces of string 24" (60 cm) long*
- two small paper cups*
- scissors
- student activity sheet*

**Procedure:**

1. Using your scissors, poke a small hole in the bottom of each paper cup. Make sure it is big enough for the string to fit through.

2. Take one piece of string and thread it through the hole. Once it is threaded, tie a knot on the inside of the cup big enough so the string will not come through when pulled. Repeat this on the second cup.

3. When your cups are ready, tie the free ends of the strings to the opposite ends of the hanger.

4. Hold the cups up to your ears and hit the hanger against a solid object. Listen to the sound that is made.

5. Try hitting the hanger against several different types of objects to see if there is a difference.

6. Complete the attached activity sheet and return it and any unused school supplies on the date due.

**Why:** When the hanger is hit against a solid object, sounds are created. You hear them so well because they are able to travel up the string, through the cup, and into your ears.

# Sound Waves (cont.)

## Introduction and Follow-up Activities

### Setting the Stage

- See if any your students can explain what sound waves are.

- Ask students why they think they can hear different sounds.

- Ask students if there are certain sounds they cannot hear.

- Have students define the term *vibration*.

- Pass out science kits and explain to students what they will be investigating at home.

### Extensions

- Review with students the results of their home investigations.

- In class have students choose partners; give each pair two paper cups and a piece of string 13' (4 m) long. Have them poke a small hole in the bottom of each cup with a pair of scissors, thread the string through each hole, and tie a knot on the inside of the cups. Then, have them stretch the string out; one person should speak into the cup while the other one listens to what is being said. Have all of the student teams interweave their strings; then have one student say something while everyone else listens.

### Closure

In a journal, have students draw a picture of sound waves going from their mouth, into the first cup, across the string, into the second cup, and finally into a partner's ear.

### Related References

Ardley, Neil. *The Science Book of Sounds.* HBJ, 1991. (3-6)

Darling, David J. *Sounds Interesting: The Science of Acoustics.* Macmillan LB, 1992. (3-6)

Kaner, Etta. *Sound Science.* Addison Wesley, 1992. (3-5)

Showers, Paul. *The Listening Walk.* Harper LB, 1991. (K-2)

Stafford, William. *The Animal That Drank up Sound.* HBJ, 1992. (K-3)

Taylor, Barbara. *Sound and Music.* Watts LB, 1990. (3-6)

# Paper Passage

**Date Due:** _____

**Directions:** Draw a picture and then explain in your own words what happened during your investigation.

Student's Name: _____

Parent's Signature: _____

---

# Paper Passage

**Purpose:** Finding out how you can step through a piece of paper while it is still intact.

**Materials:**
- several pieces of notebook or copier paper 8.5" x 11" (22 cm x 28 cm)*
- pair of scissors
- student activity sheet*

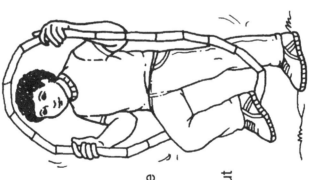

**Procedure:**

1. Using a piece of paper and scissors, make a hole in the paper large enough to walk through. You may not cut the paper up and then glue or tape it back together.

2. You may need several tries until you are able to figure out this puzzle.

3. Complete the attached activity sheet and return it and any unused school supplies on the date due.

**Why:** This activity will give you hands-on experience of how a rubber molecule works. Rubber molecules are attached at their ends, but not in the middle. This allows you to stretch the paper, and yet at the same time it will stay connected.

# Paper Passage (cont.)

## Instructions for Paper Passage

1.  Fold the paper in half. Following the pattern shown, cut a 1/2" (1.25 cm) strip from the center fold.

2.  With the paper folded, make several cuts from the center portion of the paper toward the edge. Stop cutting about 1/2" (1.25 cm) from the edge.

3.  Starting at the opposite edges from the fold, cut slits in between the first set of slits. (See illustration below.) End cuts about 1/2" (1.25 cm) from the center portion of the paper.

4.  Carefully pull apart the paper, and a large circle unfolds.

**1**

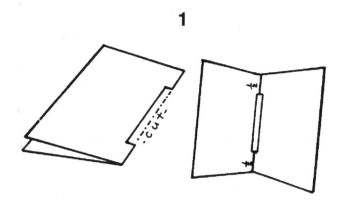

**2**

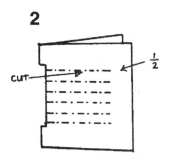

**3**

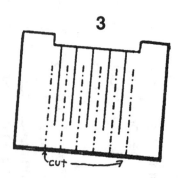

**4**

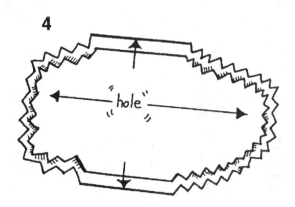

**Note to the teacher:** You may wish to send a sealed set of instructions home for parents.

# Paper Passage (cont.)

## Introduction and Follow-up Activities

### Setting the Stage

- Explain to students the activity they will be taking part in is an exercise in problem solving.

- Explain to students the properties of a rubber molecule.

- Pass out science kits and explain to students what they will be investigating at home.

### Extensions

- Review with students the results of their home investigations.

- Have students share and compare their problem-solving strategies as they attempt to create a "paper passage."

- Make sure that all students know how to make a paper passage.

- Have a class contest to see who can make the largest hole with the smallest piece of paper.

### Closure

In a journal, have students draw a picture of themselves walking through their paper passages.

### Related References

Cobb, Vicki. *Why Can't You Unscramble an Egg? And Other Not Such Dumb Questions About Matter.* Dutton, 1993. (3-6)

Cooper, Christopher. *Matter.* Dorling LB, 1992. (4-6)

Evans, David & Claudette Williams. *Make It Change.* Darling, 1992. (1-4)

# Science Activity Sheet

**Date Due:** _____

**Directions:** Draw a picture and then explain in your own words what happened during your investigation.

Student's Name: _____

Parent's Signature: _____

# Science Activity Sheet

**Purpose:**

**Materials:**

**Procedure:**

**Why:**

# Science Activity Sheet (cont.)

## Introduction and Follow-up Activities

**Setting the Stage**

**Extensions**

**Closure**

# Awards

## Super Scientist Award

This is to certify that

_____

*Name*

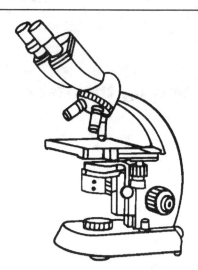

completed a science activity.

Congratulations!

_____

*Teacher*

_____

*Date*

## Special Discovery Award

This is to certify that

_____

*Name*

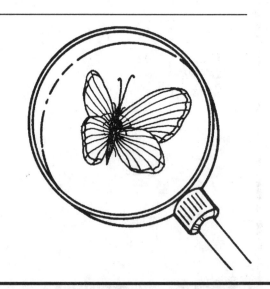

made a special discovery.

Congratulations!

_____

*Teacher*

_____

*Date*